Democracy In France
January, 1849

by

Monsieur Guizot

ABOUT THE AUTHOR

François Pierre Guillaume Guizot was a French historian, orator, and politician. Prior to the 1848 Revolution, Guizot was a dominating force in French politics. He was a conservative liberal who rejected King Charles X's effort to steal legislative power and tried to preserve a constitutional monarchy after the July Revolution of 1830. He then served the "citizen king" Louis Philippe as Minister of Education from 1832 to 1837, ambassador to London, Foreign Minister from 1840 to 1847, and lastly Prime Minister of France from September 19, 1847, to February 23, 1848. Guizot's influence was important in spreading public education, and under his government, primary schools were established in every French commune. As a leader of the "Doctrinaires," who were committed to supporting Louis Phillipe's policies and limiting further expansion of the political franchise, he earned the ire of more left-leaning liberals and republicans for his unwavering support for restricting suffrage to propertied men and allegedly advising those who wanted the vote to "enrich themselves" through hard work and thrift.

CONTENTS

CHAPTER I
WHAT IS THE SOURCE OF
THE PREVALENT EVIL?

Mirabeau, Barnave, Napoleon, and Lafayette, who died at distant and very dissimilar periods, in bed or on the scaffold, in their own country or in exile, all died under the influence of one sentiment—a sentiment of profound melancholy. They thought their hopes deceived, their labours abortive. They were assailed by doubts of the success of their cause, and by misgivings as to the future.

King Louis-Philippe reigned above seventeen years, for more than eleven of which I had the honour to be his minister. If to-morrow it pleased God to summon us into his presence, should we quit this earth very confident in the future destiny and the constitutional order of our country?

Is then the French Revolution destined to give birth only to doubt and deception?—to bury all its triumphs under ruins?

Yes: so long as France shall suffer the true and the false, the upright and the perverse, the practicable and the chimerical, the salutary and the pestilent to be constantly mingled and confounded in her opinions, her institutions, and the government of her affairs, such will be the unfailing and inevitable result.

Until a people which has gone through a great revolution has passed on the principles, the passions, and the doctrines which have led to this revolution, a sentence like that which shall be passed on all human things at the Last Day, "severing the wheat from the tares, and the corn from the straw that shall be cast into the fire," it can never surmount the perils, nor reap the advantages, of the struggle in which it has been engaged.

So long as this judgment is deferred, chaos reigns; and chaos, if prolonged in the midst of a people, would be death.

Chaos is now concealed under one word—Democracy.

This is now the sovereign and universal word which all parties invoke, all seek to appropriate as a talisman.

The Monarchists say, "Our Monarchy is a Democratic Monarchy: therefore it differs essentially from the ancient Monarchy, and is adapted to the modern condition of society."

The Republicans say, "The Republic is Democracy governing itself. This is the only form of government in harmony with a democratic society, its principles, its sentiments, and its interests."

Socialists, Communists, and Montagnards require that the republic should be a pure and absolute democracy. This, in their estimation, is the condition of its legitimacy.

Such is the power of the word Democracy, that no government or party dares to raise its head, or believes its own existence possible, if it does not bear that word inscribed on its banner; and those who carry that banner aloft with the greatest ostentation and to the extremest limits, believe themselves to be stronger than all the rest of the world.

Fatal idea, which incessantly excites and foments social war amongst us! This idea must be extirpated; for on its extirpation depends social peace, and, in her train, liberty, security, prosperity, dignity, all the benefits, material or moral, which social peace alone can ensure.

The following are the causes to which the word *democracy* owes its power.

It is the banner of all the social hopes and ambitions of man,—pure or impure, noble or base, rational or irrational, possible or chimerical.

Now it is the glory of man to be ambitious. He alone, of all created beings, does not passively resign himself to evil; he alone incessantly aspires after good; not only for himself, but for his fellow-creatures. He respects and loves the race to which he belongs; he wishes to find a remedy for their miseries, and redress for their wrongs.

But man is no less imperfect than he is ambitious. Amidst his ardent and unceasing struggles to eradicate evil and to achieve good, every one of his virtuous inclinations is accompanied by an evil inclination which treads closely on its heels, or strives with it for precedence. The desire for justice and the desire for vengeance—the spirit of liberty and the spirit of tyranny—the wish to rise and the wish to abase what has risen—the ardent love of truth and the presumptuous temerity of fancied knowledge;—we may fathom all the depths of human nature; we shall find throughout, the same mingled yet conflicting qualities, the same danger from their close and easy approximation.

To all these instincts, at once contrary and parallel,—to all indiscriminately, the bad as well as the good,—the word *Democracy* holds out an interminable vista and infinite promises. It fosters every propensity, it speaks to every passion, of the heart of man; to the most generous and the most shameful, the most moral and the most immoral, the gentlest and the harshest, the most beneficent and the most destructive: to the former it loudly offers, to the latter it secretly and dimly promises, satisfaction.

Such is the secret of its power.

I am wrong in saying, the secret. The word *Democracy* is not new, and in all ages it has signified what it signifies now. But what is new and proper to our times is this: the word *Democracy* is now pronounced every day, every hour, and in every place; and at every time and place it is heard by all men. This formidable appeal to all that is most potent, for good and for evil, in man and in society, was formerly heard only transiently, locally, and among certain classes, which, though bound to other classes by the ties of a common country, were distinct and profoundly different from them. They lived at a distance from each other; each obscurely known to the other. Now there is but one society; and in this society there are no more lofty barriers, no more great distances, no more mutual obscurities. Whether it be false or true, noxious or salutary, when once a social idea arises, it penetrates everywhere, and its action is universal and constant. It is a torch that is never extinguished; a voice that is never wearied or hushed. Universality and publicity are from henceforth the conditions of all the great provocations addressed to men,—of all the great impulses given to society.

This is doubtless one of those absolute and sovereign facts which enter into the designs of God with regard to mankind.

Such being the fact, the empire of the word *Democracy* is not to be regarded as a transitory or local accident. It is the development—others would say the explosion—of all the elements of human nature throughout all the ranks and all the depths of society; and consequently the open, general, continuous, inevitable struggle of its good and evil instincts; of its virtues and its vices; of all its powers and faculties, whether to improve or to corrupt, to raise or to abase, to create or to destroy. Such is, from henceforth, the social state, the permanent condition of our nation.

CHAPTER II
WHAT IS THE DUTY OF GOVERNMENT WITH RESPECT TO DEMOCRACY?

There are men whom this fearful struggle does not alarm: they have full confidence in human nature. According to them, if left to itself, its progress is towards good: all the evils of society arise from governments which debase men by violence or corrupt them by fraud: liberty—liberty for everybody and everything—liberty will almost always suffice to enlighten or to control the wills of men, to prevent evil or to cure it: a little government—the least possible—may be allowed for the repression of extreme disorder and the control of brute force.

Others have a more summary way of disposing of all dread of the triumph of evil in man or in society. There is, they say, no such thing as natural and necessary evil, since no human inclination is bad in itself; it becomes so, only when it does not attain the end after which it aspires—it is a torrent which overflows its banks when obstructed. If society were organized in such a manner that each of the instincts of man found its proper place and received its due satisfaction, evil would disappear, strife would cease, and all the various forces of humanity, harmoniously combine to produce social order.

The former of these speculators misunderstand man; the latter misunderstand man, and deny God.

Let any man dive into his own heart and observe himself with attention. If he have the power to look, and the will to see, he will behold, with a sort of terror, the incessant war waged by the good and evil dispositions within him—reason and caprice, duty and passion; in short, to call them all by their comprehensive names, good and evil. We contemplate with anxiety the outward troubles and vicissitudes of human life; but what should we feel if we could behold the inward vicissitudes, the troubles of the human soul?—if we could see how many dangers, snares, enemies, combats, victories, and defeats can be crowded into a day—an hour? I do not say this to discourage man, nor to humble or under-value his free will. He is called upon to conquer in the battle of life, and the honour of the conquest belongs to his free will. But victory is impossible, and defeat certain, if he has not a just conception and a profound feeling of his dangers, his weaknesses, and his need of assistance. To believe that the free will of man tends to good, and is of itself sufficient to accomplish good, betrays an immeasurable ignorance of his nature. It is the error of pride; an error which tends to destroy both moral and political order; which enfeebles the government of communities no less than the government of the inward man.

For the struggle is the same, the peril as imminent, the aid as necessary, in society as in the individual man. Many of those now living have been doomed to see, several times in the course of their lives, the social edifice tottering to its fall, and all the props that should uphold, all the bonds that should unite it, failing. Over what an immense extent, and with what fearful rapidity, have all the causes of social war and social destruction, which are always fermenting in the midst of us, each time burst forth! Which of us has not shuddered at the sudden discovery of the abyss over which we live—the frail barriers which separate us from it, and the destructive legions ready to rush forth upon society as soon as its jaws are unclosed? For my own part, I was a spectator, day by day, hour by hour, of the purest, the wisest, the gentlest, and the shortest of these formidable convulsions; in July, 1830, I saw, in the streets and the palaces, at the gate of the national councils and in the midst of popular assemblies, society abandoned to itself, an actor or spectator of the revolution. And at the same time that I admired the generous sentiments, the proofs of strong intelligence and disinterested virtue and heroic moderation which I witnessed, I shuddered as I saw a mighty torrent of insensate ideas, brutal passions, perverse inclinations, and terrible chimeras, rise and swell, minute by minute, ready to overflow, and submerge a land where all the dikes that had contained it were broken down. Society had gloriously repulsed the violation of its laws and its honour, and now it was on the point of falling into ruins in the midst of its glory. Here it was that I learned the vital conditions of social order, and the necessity of resistance to ensure the safety of the social fabric.

Resistance not only to evil, but to the principle of evil; not only to disorder, but to the passions and the ideas which engender disorder—this is the paramount and peremptory duty of every government. And the greater the empire of Democracy, the more important is it that government should hold fast to its true character, and act its true part in the struggle which agitates society. Why is it that so many democracies—some of them very brilliant—have so rapidly perished? Because they would not suffer their governments to do their duty, and fulfil the objects for which governments are instituted. They did more than reduce them to weakness; they condemned them to falsehood. It is the melancholy condition of democratic governments, that while charged—as they must be—with the repression of disorder, they are required to be complaisant and indulgent to the causes of disorder; they are expected to arrest the evil when it breaks out, and yet they are asked to foster it whilst it is hatching. I know no more deplorable spectacle than a power which, in the struggle between the good and the evil principle, continually bends the knee before the bad, and then attempts to resume an attitude of vigour and independence when it becomes necessary to resist its excesses. If you will not have excesses, you must repress them in their origin. If you wish for liberty—for the full and glorious development of human nature—learn first on what conditions this is attainable; look forward to its consequences. Do not blind yourselves to the perils and the combats it will occasion. And when these combats and these perils arise, do not require your leaders to be hypocritical or weak in their dealings with the enemy. Do not force upon them the worship of idols, even were you yourselves those idols. Permit them, nay command them, to worship and to serve the true God alone.

I might here allow myself the satisfaction of recalling the names of all the rulers who have fallen shamefully because they submitted basely to be the slaves or the tools of the errors and passions of the democracies it was their duty and their vocation to govern; but I had rather dwell on the memory of those who lived gloriously by resisting them. It is more to my taste to prove the truth by examples of the success which crowns wisdom, than by those of the disasters which attend on folly.

Democratic France owes much to the Emperor Napoleon. He gave her two things of immense value: within, civil order strongly constituted; without, national independence firmly established. But had she ever a government which treated her with greater severity, or showed less complaisance for the favourite passions of Democracy? As to the political constitution of the state, Napoleon's only care was to raise power from the abasement into which it had fallen, to restore to it all the conditions of force and greatness. In this he saw a national interest paramount to all others, whether the nation were governed democratically or otherwise.

But Napoleon was a despot. If he rightly understood and ably served some of the great interests of that new France he had to govern, he profoundly misunderstood and injured others, not less sacred. How was it possible that one so hostile to liberty should be favourable to the political propensities of Democracy?

I shall not contest this. I run no risk of forgetting that Napoleon was a despot, for I have not to learn it now—I thought so when he was living. It may, however, be asked whether he could have been otherwise? whether he could have tolerated political liberty, and whether we were then in a state to receive it? I shall not attempt to decide these questions. There are men, and very great men, who are suited to certain diseased and transitory crises, and not to the sane and permanent state, of society. Napoleon was, perhaps, one of those men. That he mistook some of the essential wants of our time, nobody is more convinced than I am. But he re-established order and authority in the midst of democratic France. He believed, and he proved, that it was possible to serve and to govern a democratic society without humouring all its inclinations. This is his real greatness.

Washington has no resemblance to Napoleon. He was not a despot. He founded the political liberty, at the same time as the national independence, of his country. He used war only as a means to peace. Raised to the supreme power without ambition, he descended from it without regret, as soon as the safety of his country permitted. He is the model for all democratic chiefs. Now you have only to examine his life, his soul, his acts, his thoughts, his words; you will not find a single mark of condescension, a single moment of indulgence, for the favourite ideas of Democracy. He constantly struggled—struggled even to weariness and to sadness—against its exactions. No man was ever more profoundly imbued with the spirit of government, or with respect for authority. He never exceeded the rights of power, according to the laws of his country; but he confirmed and maintained them, in principle as well as in practice, as firmly, as loftily, as he could have done in an old monarchical or aristocratical state. He was one of those who knew that it is no more possible to govern from below in a republic than in a monarchy—in a democratic than in an aristocratic society.

Democratic societies enjoy no privilege which renders the spirit of government less necessary in them than in others; no privilege which renders their vital conditions different or inferior to those required elsewhere. By an infallible consequence of the struggle which infallibly arises in such societies, the possessor of power is continually called on to decide between the contrary impulses by which he is solicited to make himself the artisan of good or the accomplice of evil, the champion of order or the slave of disorder. The mythic story of the choice of Hercules is the daily and hourly history of his life. Every government, whatever be its form or its name, which, by the vice of its organization or situation, or by the corruption or feebleness of its will, cannot fulfil this inevitable task, will speedily pass away like an evil phantom, or will ruin the democracy it affects to establish.

CHAPTER III
OF THE DEMOCRATIC REPUBLIC

I shall not speak of the republican form of government otherwise than with respect. Considered in itself, it is a noble form of government. It has called forth great virtues; it has presided over the destiny and the glory of great nations.

But a republican government has the same vocation, the same duties, as any other government. Its name gives it no claim to dispensation or privilege. It must satisfy both the general and permanent wants of human society, and the particular wants of the particular community which it is called to govern.

The permanent want of every community,—the first and most imperious want of France at the present day,—is, peace in the bosom of society itself.

A great deal has been said about unity and social fraternity. These are sublime words, but they ought not to make us forget facts. Nothing has a more certain tendency to ruin a people than a habit of accepting words and appearances as realities. Whilst the shouts of unity and fraternity resound among us, they are responded to by social war, flagrant or imminent, terrible from the evils it causes, or from those it seems likely to cause.

I will not dwell on this grievous wound. Yet in order to cure, we ought to touch, and even to probe it. It is an old wound. The history of France is filled with the struggle between the different classes of society, of which the Revolution of 1789 was the most general and mighty explosion. The contests between nobility and commonalty, aristocracy and democracy, masters and workmen, those possessing property and those dependent on wages, are all different forms and phases of the social struggle which has so long agitated France. And it is at the very moment when we are boasting of having reached the summit of civilization—it is while the most humane words that can issue from the lips of man are ringing in our ears, that this struggle is revived more violently, more fiercely than ever!

This is a curse and a shame, of which we, and the age we live in, must rid ourselves. Internal peace, peace among all classes of citizens, is the paramount want, the only chance for the salvation of France.

Will the Democratic Republic give us this peace?

It did not begin well. When scarcely born, a civil war was its first necessity—most unfortunately for the republic. Governments find great difficulty in rising out of their cradles. Will the Democratic Republic succeed in the attempt? If time is allowed to it, will it restore social peace?

There is one circumstance which strikes me powerfully, and causes me great anxiety: that is, the ardour manifested by the republic to be expressly and officially called democratic.

The United States of America are universally admitted to be the model of a Republic and a Democracy. Did it ever enter the head of the American people to call the United States a Democratic Republic?

No; nor is this astonishing. In that country there was no struggle between Aristocracy and Democracy; between an ancient aristocratical society and a new democratic society: on the contrary, the leaders of society in the United States, the descendants of the first colonists, the majority of the principal planters in the country and the principal merchants in the towns, who constituted the natural aristocracy of the country, placed themselves at the head of the revolution and the republic. The devotion, energy, and constancy which they showed in the cause, were greater than those displayed by the people. The conquest of their independence, and the foundation of the republic, was not, then, the work and the victory of certain classes over certain other classes; it was the joint work of all, led by the highest, the wealthiest, and the most enlightened, who had often great difficulty in rallying the spirit and sustaining the courage of the mass of the population.

Whenever officers were to be chosen for the bodies of troops formed in the several States, Washington gave this advice:—"Take none but gentlemen: they are the most trustworthy, as well as the ablest."

A republican government has more need than any other of the co-operation of every class of its citizens: if the mass of the population does not zealously adopt it, it has no root; if the higher classes are hostile or indifferent to it, it can enjoy no security. In either case, it is reduced to the necessity of oppressing. It is precisely because in a republic the authority of the government is weak and precarious, that it stands in need of great moral support from the society over which it presides. Which are the republics that have lived long and honourably, overcoming the defects and the storms incident to their institutions? Those only in which the republican spirit was sincere and general; which obtained, on the one side, the attachment and the confidence of the people, and on the other the decided support of the classes who, by their position, fortune, education, and habits, bring into public life the largest share of natural authority, tranquil independence, knowledge, and leisure. On these conditions only can a republic be established or maintained; for on these conditions only can it exist without troubling the peace of society, and without condemning its government to the deplorable alternative of the disorganization of anarchy, or the rigid tension of tyranny.

The United States of America enjoyed this singular good fortune, but it is denied to the French Republic. Indeed this is not only admitted, but proclaimed and vaunted, by its authors. What is the meaning of the words *Democratic Republic* now current amongst us, and adopted as the official name, the symbol of the government? It is the echo of an ancient social war-cry—a cry which is still raised, still repeated in every class of society; still angrily uttered against one class by another, which, in its turn, hears it with terror directed against itself. All are in turn democrats as against those above them, aristocrats as against those below; threatening and threatened, envious or envied, and exhibiting continual and revolting changes of position, attitude, and language, and a deplorable confusion of conflicting ideas and passions. It is war in the midst of chaos.

But I hear it said, "This war is a fact—it is the dominant fact of our history, our society, and our revolution. Such facts can neither be hidden nor passed over in silence, and this is become final and decisive. It is not war that we proclaimed in proclaiming a Democratic Republic, it is victory— the victory of Democracy. Democracy has conquered, and remains alone on the field of battle. She raises her visor, announces her name, and takes possession of her conquest."

Such an answer is dictated by illusion or by hypocrisy. How does a government, whether democratic or not, assert and prove its victory, when that victory is real and decisive? By restoring peace. Thus, and thus alone, could the Democratic Republic have proved that it had conquered. But does peace reign in France? Is it even approaching? Do the various elements of society, willingly or unwillingly, satisfied or resigned, really believe in the existence and permanence of peace, and come to seek tranquillity, order, and protection under the shelter of the Democratic Republic? Listen to the comments on the title assumed by the republican government which are universally heard; see the striking and menacing facts which are continually occurring, and which are the consequence or the proof of those comments. Is this state of things peace? Is there, I will not say the reality, but the bare appearance, of one of those energetic, wise, and conclusive victories which put an end, for a time at least, to social conflicts, and secure a long truce to harassed nations?

There are facts of such magnitude, clearness, and prominence, that no human force or fraud can succeed in hiding them. It is in vain that you repeat that the days of fraternity are come; that Democracy, such as you establish it, puts an end to all hostilities or conflicts of classes, and assimilates and unites all orders of citizens. The truth, the terrible truth, gleams through these vain words. Interests, passions, pretensions, situations, and classes conflict on every side, with all the fury of boundless hopes and boundless fears. It is clear that the first acts of the Democratic Republic threaten to plunge herself and us into the chaos of social war.

And does she give us arms for our defence, or open to us issues for our escape?

I pass over the name she assumes; I turn to the political ideas she proclaims as laws for the government of the state: so far from diminishing my anxiety, these serve but to increase it. For if the banner of the Democratic Republic appears to me to bear the inscription of social war, its constitution seems to me to lead directly to revolutionary despotism. I find in it no distinct powers, possessed of sufficient inherent strength to exercise a reciprocal control; no solid ramparts, under the shelter of which various rights and interests can take root and flourish in safety; no organization of guarantees; no balance of powers in the centre of the state and at the head of government—nothing but a single motive force and various wheels; a master and his agents; nothing between the personal liberty of the citizens and the bare will of the numerical majority: the principle of despotism, checked by the right of insurrection.

Such is the position of the Democratic Republic with relation to social order; such, with relation to political order, is the government which it constitutes.

What can be the result? Assuredly neither peace nor liberty.

When the republic was proclaimed, in the midst of general and profound alarm, one sentiment prevailed. A great number of men attached to the interests of their country, said, or thought, "Let us wait; let us try— perhaps the republic will be different now from what it was heretofore; let the experiment be tried—let it not be disturbed by violence: we shall see the result."

They kept their word; they have excited no troubles, they have raised no obstacles, to disturb or to impede the progress of the republic.

The same sentiment prevailed throughout Europe—a sentiment inspired, no doubt, by prudence, and not by any cordiality or hope: but the motives which influenced Europe signify little; the important fact is, that no act, no danger from without troubles the French Republic in the experiment of its foundation.

On the other hand, justice compels us to acknowledge that the leaders of the republic have endeavoured to belie the predictions of its adversaries and the fears of the public. They have respected the faith of men. They have fought—very late, it is true, but at last they have fought—for the existence of society. They have not broken the peace of Europe, and they have striven to maintain the public credit. These meritorious efforts do honour to the men invested with power, and show, moreover, what the general instincts of the country are. But these men can only retard, they cannot arrest, the downward course of the state on a fatal declivity; they can find no firm footing, and lose ground at every step. They have sunk into the revolutionary rut; and though they struggle not to plunge deeper into it, they cannot, or they dare not, quit it. The acts of the republic are not, in all points, what they formerly were; but the republic is what it was. Whether as to social organization or political institutions, the conditions of order or the securities for liberty, the republic has nothing better to offer than what she offered fifty years ago. There are the same ideas, the same crude and rash experiments, often even the same forms and the same words. Strange spectacle! The authors of the republic are afraid of their own work, and would fain change its character and aspect; but they can produce nothing but a copy.

How long, whatever be its ultimate success or failure, the present attempt will last, nobody knows. But hitherto France has evidently reason to fear that its first and paramount interests—social peace and political liberty—will be placed, or left, by the Democratic Republic, in immense danger.

CHAPTER IV
OF THE SOCIAL REPUBLIC

The Social Republic promises to solve the difficulty.

"All systems, all governments," it declares, "have been tried and found wanting. My ideas alone are new, and have not yet been put to the test. My day is come."

This is a mistake. The ideas propounded by the Social Republic are not new. They are as old as the world. They have risen up in the midst of all the great moral and social crises, whether in the East or the West, in the ancient or the modern world. The second and third centuries in Africa, and especially in Egypt, during the agitations caused by the propagation of Christianity — the middle ages during their confused, stormy fermentation — the sixteenth century in Germany, in the course of the Reformation — and the seventeenth in England during the political revolution, — had their Socialists and their Communists, thinking, speaking, and acting precisely like those of our own day. It is a phase of human nature that reappears at epochs when society is like a boiling caldron, in which every ingredient is thrown to the surface and exposed to view.

Till now, it is true, these ideas had only been enounced on a small scale, obscurely and timidly, and were repelled and execrated almost as soon as they saw the light. But now they boldly exhibit themselves, and put forth all their pretensions before the public. It signifies little whether this is by their own strength, by the fault of the public itself, or from causes inherent in the present state of society. Since the Social Republic is proclaimed aloud, we must look at it steadily and endeavour to fathom its lowest depths.

I wish to avoid all circumlocution, to throw aside all disguises, and to go straight to the heart of the idol. Nor is this impossible. For as all the efforts of the Social Republic tend to one end, so all its ideas are the offspring of one fundamental idea.

This fundamental idea is to be found, explicitly or implicitly, in the language of all the leaders of the Social Republic, though all do not avow, and some are perhaps not even conscious that they entertain it. M. Proudhon appears to me the one among them who knows best what he thinks and what he wishes: he appears to show the firmest and most consistent understanding in his detestable dreams.

It is not, however, so firm nor so consistent as it appears, or probably as he himself thinks it. He has not declared, and I doubt if he have perceived, to what his system leads.

His system, nakedly and rigorously stated, is this:—

All men have a right—and the same right—to happiness.

Happiness is the enjoyment (without any limit but that prescribed by the want and the faculty of enjoying) of all the good things existing or possible in this world; whether natural and primitive, or progressively created by the intelligence and the labour of man.

Certain men, certain families, or certain classes have acquired the exclusive enjoyment of some (indeed the greater part) of the most essential and productive of these good things; or, in other words, these things, or the means of procuring them, are become the special and perpetual property of certain men, families, and classes.

Such a confiscation of a part of the fund common to mankind, for the advantage of a few, is essentially contrary to justice; contrary to the rights of the men of the same generation, who ought all to enjoy it equally; and contrary to the rights of successive generations, each of which, on its entrance into life, ought to find the good things of life equally accessible, and to enjoy them in its turn like its predecessors.

Therefore all special and perpetual appropriation of the good things which confer happiness, and of the means of procuring those good things, must be abolished, in order to insure the universal enjoyment and the equal distribution of them amongst all men, and all successive generations of men.

But how is it possible to abolish property? or, at least, so to transform it, that, as regards its social and permanent effects, it may be as if it were abolished?

Here the leaders of the Social Republic differ greatly among themselves. Some recommend slow and gentle measures; others urge prompt and decisive ones. Some have recourse to political means—for example, a certain organization of existence and labour in common; others try to invent economical and financial expedients—for example, a series of measures designed gradually to destroy the net revenue of property, whether in land or capital, and thus to render property itself useless and illusory. But all these schemes originate in the same design and tend to the same result; the abolition or the nullification of personal, domestic, and hereditary property; and of all institutions, social or political, which are based upon personal, domestic, and hereditary property.

Such, through all the diversity, obscurity, ambiguity, and contradiction of the ideas which circulate among the adherents of the Social Republic, is the beginning and the end, the alpha and omega, of all these systems; such is the end they pursue, and hope to attain.

But the following truths are forgotten by M. Proudhon and his friends.

Mankind is not merely a series of individuals called men; it is a race, which has a common life, and a general and progressive destiny. This is the distinctive character of man, which he alone of created beings possesses.

And why is this? It is because human individuals are not isolated, nor confined to themselves, and to the point they occupy in space or time. They are connected with each other; they act upon each other, by ties and by means which do not require their presence, and which outlive them. Hence the successive generations of men are linked together in unbroken succession.

The permanent union and progressive development which are the consequences of this unbroken succession of man to man, and generation to generation, characterize the human race. They constitute its peculiarity and its greatness, and mark man for sovereignty in this world, and for immortality beyond it.

From this are derived, and by this are founded, the family and the state, property and inheritance, country, history, glory, all the facts and all the sentiments which constitute the extended and perpetual life of mankind, amidst the bounded appearance and rapid disappearance of individual men.

In the Social Republic all this ceases to exist. Men are mere isolated and ephemeral beings, who appear in this life, and on this earth the scene of life, only to take their subsistence and their pleasure, each for himself alone, each by the same right, and without any end or purpose beyond.

This is precisely the condition of the lower animals. Among them there exists no tie, no influence, which survives the individual, and extends to the race. There is no permanent appropriation, no hereditary transmission, no unity nor progress in the life of the species;—nothing but individuals who appear and then vanish, seizing on their passage their portion of the good things of the earth and the pleasures of life, according to the combined measure of their wants and their strength, which, according to them, constitute their right.

Thus, in order to secure to every individual of the human species the equal and incessantly fluctuating share of the goods and pleasures of sense, the doctrines of the Social Republic bring men down to the level of the lower animals. They obliterate the human race.

They do worse.

There is in the mind of man an imperishable instinct that God presides over his destiny, and that it is not wholly accomplished in this world. Naturally and universally, man believes in God and invokes him as his support in the present, his hope in the future.

According to the doctrines of the Social Republic, God is an unknown imaginary power, upon whom the visible and real rulers of men upon earth throw the weight of their own responsibility, and by thus directing the eyes of the suffering towards another master and another state of existence, dispose them to acquiesce in their afflictions, whilst they secure themselves in the maintenance of their usurpations. According then to this doctrine, God is evil, for it is in his name that men are persuaded to acquiesce in evil. To banish evil from the earth, it therefore is necessary to banish God from the mind of man. Men left alone with their earthly masters, and reduced to an earthly existence, will demand the enjoyments of this life and the equal distribution of these enjoyments; and as soon as those who are without them insist on having them, they will have them, for they are the strongest.

Thus God and the human race will disappear together. In their place will remain animals still bearing the name of men, more intelligent and more powerful than other animals, but having the same condition and the same destiny; and like them seizing, on their passage through life, their portion of the goods of earth and the pleasures of sense, according to the combined measure of their wants and their strength, which constitute their right.

Such is the philosophy of the Social Republic; such, therefore, is the basis of its policy. We have traced its origin and its end.

I will not insult the good sense or the dignity of mankind by dwelling on it longer. It is the degradation of man, and the destruction of society.

Not only of society as at present constituted, but of all human society whatsoever: for all society rests on foundations which it is the object of the Social Republic to overthrow. It is not a mere invasion of the social edifice by intruders, whether barbarian or not; it is the utter ruin of the edifice itself that is contemplated. If M. Proudhon had the absolute disposal of society in its present state, with all that it possesses or enjoys, and were to change the distribution and the possessors of property at his own good pleasure, he would be guilty of great iniquity, and occasion great suffering. He would not, however, destroy society. But if he pretended to give the ideas with which he tries to batter down the present structure of society, as laws to one newly framed, it would infallibly perish. Instead of a State and a People, there would be only a chaos of human beings, without a tie and without repose. Nor would it be possible to reduce that chaos to order without abandoning or evading the ideas of the Social Republic, and returning to the natural conditions of social order.

The Social Republic is then at once odious and impossible. It is the most absurd, and at the same time the most perverse, of all chimeras.

But we must not presume upon this. Nothing is more dangerous than what is at once strong and impossible. The Social Republic is strong; indeed how can it be otherwise? Availing themselves with ardour of every kind of liberty granted for the promulgation of ideas, its advocates are incessantly labouring to diffuse their principles and their promises through the densest ranks of society. There they find masses of men easy to delude, easy to inflame. They offer them rights in conformity with their desires. They excite their passions in the name of justice and truth. For it would be puerile to deny (and for the honour of human nature we must admit) that the ideas of the Social Republic have, to many minds, the character and the force of truth. In questions so complex and so exciting, the smallest gleam of truth is sufficient to dazzle the eyes and inflame the hearts of men, and to dispose them to embrace with transport the grossest and most fatal errors with which that truth is blended. Fanaticism is kindled at the same time that selfishness is awakened; sincere devotedness joins hands with brutal passions; and, in the terrible fermentation which ensues, evil predominates; the portion of good mingled with it acts only as its veil and its instrument.

We have no right to complain, for it is we ourselves who incessantly add fuel to the fire—and this is the most deep-seated of our maladies. It is we who give to the Social Republic its chief strength. It is the chaos of our political ideas and our political morality—that chaos disguised sometimes under the word *democracy*, sometimes under that of *equality*, sometimes under that of *people*—which opens all the gates, and throws down all the ramparts of society before it. We say that Democracy is everything. The men of the Social Republic reply, "Democracy is ourselves." We proclaim, in language of infinite confusion, the absolute equality of rights and the sovereign right of numbers. The men of the Social Republic come forward and say, "Count our numbers." The perpetual confusion of the true and the false, the good and the bad, the possible and the chimerical, which prevails in our own policy, our own language, our own acts—this it is which has enfeebled our arm for defence, and given to the Social Republic a confidence, an arrogance, and an influence for attack, which of itself it would never possess.

When this confusion shall be dissipated; when we shall arrive at that period of maturity in which free nations, instead of blindly following their first impressions, whithersoever they may lead, see things as they really are, assign to the different elements of society their just measure, and to words their true meaning, and regulate their ideas as they do their affairs, with that firm moderation which rejects all fantasies, admits all necessities, respects all rights, has regard to all interests, and represses all usurpations;—those from below no less than those from above—those of fanaticism no less than those of selfishness: when we shall have reached this point, although the Social Republic may not entirely disappear, and although we may not have entirely crushed its efforts nor annihilated its dangers (for it derives its ambition and its strength from sources that none can dry up), still it will be controlled by the union and the order of society; all that is most absurd and perverse in its doctrines will be incessantly combated and defeated, and it will in time take its due place in that vast and imposing development of the human race which is passing before our eyes.

CHAPTER V
WHAT ARE THE REAL AND ESSENTIAL ELEMENTS OF SOCIETY IN FRANCE?

The first step towards extricating ourselves out of the chaos in which we are plunged, is, a full understanding and frank admission of all the real and essential elements of which society in France is now composed.

It is because we misunderstand these elements, or refuse them the place and the consideration they deserve, that we remain in, or relapse into, chaos.

A society may be tortured, perhaps destroyed; but you cannot force it to assume a form and mode of existence foreign to its nature, either by disregarding the essential elements of which it is constituted, or by doing violence to them.

Let us first advert to that civil order which forms the basis of French society, as of every other society.

Family; property of all kinds, whether land, capital, or wages; labour, under all its forms, individual or collective, intellectual or manual; the situations in which men are placed, or the relations which are introduced among them by the incidents of family, property, and labour;—such are the constituents of civil society.

The essential and characteristic fact in French civil society is, unity of laws and equality of rights. All families, property of every kind, labour of every description, are governed by the same laws, and possess or confer the same civil rights. There are no privileges; that is, no laws or rights peculiar to particular families, or to property or labour of particular sorts.

This is a new and mighty fact in the history of human societies.

But notwithstanding this fact, notwithstanding this civil unity and equality, there are evidently numerous and great diversities and inequalities, which unity of laws and equality of rights can neither prevent nor remove.

As to property, whether in immoveables or moveables, land or capital, there are rich and poor; there are large, middling, and small properties.

The great proprietors may be less numerous and less wealthy, and the middling and small proprietors may be more numerous and more powerful, than they were formerly, or than they are in other countries; but this does not prevent the inequality amongst them from being real and great enough to occasion a radical difference and inequality of social position.

From diversities of position founded on property, I pass on to those founded upon labour, of every kind and degree, from the highest intellectual, to the lowest manual labour. Here too I meet with the same fact. Here too diversity and inequality arise and subsist, in spite of identical laws and equal rights.

In the professions called liberal, or those which depend on the cultivation and employment of the intellect; among lawyers, physicians, men of science, and literary men of every sort, some few rise to the highest rank, attract business, and gain success, reputation, wealth, and influence. Others earn laboriously what is barely sufficient for the wants of their families, and the decencies of their station. Many more vegetate in obscure and unemployed indigence.

And here one fact deserves notice. From the time when all professions have been accessible to all, from the time when labour has been free, subject only to the same laws for all, the number of men who have raised themselves to the first ranks in the liberal professions has not sensibly increased. It does not appear that there are now more great lawyers or physicians, more men of science or letters of the first order, than there were formerly. It is the men of the second order, and the obscure and idle multitude, that are multiplied. It is as if Providence did not permit human laws to have any influence over the intellectual rank of its creatures, or the extent and magnificence of its gifts.

In the other trades or professions, in which labour is chiefly material and manual, there are also different and unequal situations. Some, by intelligence and good conduct, accumulate a capital and enter upon the path of competence and advancement; others, either incapable or improvident, lazy or dissolute, remain in the narrow and precarious condition of men dependent upon the daily casualties of wages.

Thus throughout the whole extent of civil society,—whether among those who depend on labour, or those possessed of property,—diversity and inequality of situation arise and coexist with unity of laws and equality of rights.

How, indeed, can it be otherwise? If we examine every form of human society throughout all ages and countries—whatever be the variety of their organization, government, extent, or duration, or of the kind and degree of civilization to which they have attained—we shall find three types of social position always fundamentally the same, though under very different forms and very differently distributed.

1. Men living on the income of their property, whether in land or capital, without seeking to increase it by their own labour;

2. Men occupied in increasing by their own labour the property, whether in land or capital, which they possess;

3. Men living by their labour without land or capital.

These diversities and inequalities in the social condition of men are not accidental, or peculiar to any particular time or country. They are universal facts, which naturally arise in every human society, amidst circumstances, and under laws, the most widely different.

And the more accurately we study them, the more clearly we shall perceive that there exists an intimate connexion and a profound harmony between these facts and the nature of man, which we know, on the one hand, and the mysteries of his destiny, of which we can only obtain a dim and distant glance, on the other.

Nor is this all. Independently of these diversities and inequalities among individuals, whether proprietors or labourers, other diversities and other inequalities exist among the kinds of property and of labour. These differences are not less real than the others, though they are less apparent; nor are they more incompatible with unity of laws or equality of civil rights.

Moveable property, or capital, has acquired, and continues to acquire, an ever increasing extension and importance in the communities of modern Europe. It is evident that the progress of civilization in our times is entirely in favour of its development; a just requital for the immense services which capital has rendered to civilization.

But this is not enough: efforts are continually made to assimilate immoveable to moveable property; to render land as transferable, as divisible, as convenient to possess and to improve as capital. All the proposed innovations, direct or indirect, in the laws relating to landed property, have this object in view, either openly or covertly.

But though a movement so favourable to capital is going on, landed property is still the most considerable in France, and still holds the first place in the estimation and the desires of the people. Those who possess it addict themselves more and more to the enjoyment of it, and those who do not possess it are more and more eager after its acquisition. The great proprietor is returning to the taste for living on his estate: the tradesman, who has earned a competence, retires to the country to enjoy repose: the peasant thinks of nothing but how to add field to field. Whilst everything is done to favour the development of capital, landed property is more in request and more prized than ever.

It may be confidently predicted that if, as I hope, social order triumphs over its insane or depraved enemies, the attacks of which landed property is now the object, and the dangers with which it is threatened, will, in the end, enhance its preponderance in society.

Whence arises this preponderance? Is it merely because, of all sorts of property, land is the most secure, the least variable;—that which best resists the perturbations, and survives the calamities of society?

This motive, though real, powerful, and obvious, is far from being the only one. There are other motives, or rather we may call them deep-seated instincts, whose empire over man is great, even when he is unconscious of it. These secure the social preponderance of landed property, or restore it when transiently shaken or enfeebled. Among these instincts two appear to me the most powerful; it will be sufficient to indicate them, for an attempt to fathom their depths would carry me too far.

Moveable property, or capital, may procure a man all the advantages of wealth; but property in land gives him much more than this. It gives him a place in the domain of the world—it unites his life to the life which animates all creation. Money is an instrument by which man can procure the satisfaction of his wants and his desires. Landed property is the establishment of man as sovereign in the midst of nature. It satisfies not only his wants and his desires, but tastes deeply implanted in his nature. For his family, it creates that domestic country called home, with all the living sympathies and all the future hopes and projects which people it. And whilst property in land is more consonant than any other to the nature of man, it also affords a field of activity the most favourable to his moral development, the most suited to inspire a just sentiment of his nature and his powers. In almost all the other trades or professions, whether commercial or scientific, success appears to depend solely on himself—on his talents, address, prudence, and vigilance. In agricultural life, man is constantly in the presence of God, and of his power. Activity, talents, prudence and vigilance are as necessary here as elsewhere to the success of his labours, but they are evidently no less insufficient than they are necessary. It is God who rules the seasons and the temperature, the sun and the rain, and all those phenomena of nature which determine the success or the failure of the labours of man on the soil which he cultivates. There is no pride which can resist this dependence, no address which can escape it. Nor is it only a sentiment of humility as to his power over his own destiny which is thus inculcated upon man; he learns also tranquillity and patience. He cannot flatter himself that the most ingenious inventions or the most restless activity will ensure his success; when he has done all that depends upon him for the cultivation and the fertilization of the soil, he must wait with resignation. The more profoundly we examine the situation in which man is placed by the possession and cultivation of the soil, the more do we discover how rich it is in salutary lessons to his reason, and benign influences on his character. Men do not analyze these facts, but they have an instinctive sentiment of them, which powerfully contributes to that peculiar respect in which they hold property in land, and to the preponderance which that kind of property enjoys over every other. This preponderance is a natural, legitimate and salutary fact, which, especially in a great country, society at large has a strong interest in recognising and respecting.

What I have just shown with relation to property, is equally true with relation to labour. It is the glory of modern civilization to have understood and proclaimed the moral value and the social importance of labour; to have raised it to the estimation and the rank which justly belong to it. If I had to point out the most profound evil, the most fatal vice, of the state of things which prevailed in France up to the sixteenth century, I should say, without hesitation, the contempt in which labour was held. Contempt of labour and pride in idleness are certain signs either that society is under the dominion of brute force, or that it is verging to its decline. Labour is the law which God has enjoined on man. It is by labour that he developes and improves everything around him—by labour that he developes and improves his own nature. Labour is become the surest pledge of peace between nations. The respect and the liberty enjoyed by labour tend more than anything to calm the anxieties which we might otherwise too justly feel, and to raise our hopes for the prospects of the human race. By what fatality then has it happened that the word *labour*, so honourable to modern civilization, is become a war-cry and a source of disasters in France? It is because that word is made a cloak for a great and pernicious lie. It is not labour, its interests or its rights, which are the object of the ferment excited in its name; the war which has been declared on the plea of protecting labour, is not in fact waged in its behalf, nor, if successful, would redound to its advantage. It is, on the contrary, directed against labour, whose ruin and degradation would be its infallible result.

Labour, like family, property, and everything else in this world, is subject to natural and general laws; among which are, diversity and inequality of the kinds and the results of labour, and of the stations of those by whom it is performed. Intellectual labour is superior to manual.

Descartes, who enlightened France, and Colbert, who laid the foundations of her prosperity, performed a labour superior to that of the workman who prints the works of Descartes, or who helps to produce the manufactures fostered by Colbert; and among these very workmen, those who are intelligent, moral, and industrious, justly attain to a situation superior to that which the same description of labour can secure to the dull, the lazy, or the licentious. The variety of tasks and vocations allotted to man is infinite. Labour is everywhere—in the house of a father of a family, who educates his children and superintends his affairs; in the cabinet of a statesman who takes part in the government of his country; in that of the magistrate who administers its laws; of the philosopher who instructs, and of the poet who charms it; in the fields, on the ocean, on the highways, in the manufactories and the workshops; and in every situation, in every variety of labour, in every class of labourers, diversity and inequality arise and subsist; inequality of intellectual power, of moral merit, of social importance, of material wealth. These are the natural, primitive, universal laws of labour, originating in the nature and condition of man, or, to speak more properly, ordained by the wisdom of God. It is against these laws that the war of which we are witnesses is waged; it is this hierarchy of labour, founded on the decrees of God and the free actions of man, which it is the object of this war to abolish; and to substitute—what?—the degradation and the ruin of labour, by the reduction of all labour and all labourers to the same level! Examine the meaning which is usually affixed to the word *labour* in the language of these enemies of social order. They do not distinctly say that material and manual work are the only real work; indeed they occasionally affect great respect for purely intellectual labour: but they omit to mention the various sorts of higher labour which are performed on every stage of the social scale; their whole attention is absorbed by material labour, which they constantly represent as the kind of labour whose importance throws every other into the shade. In short, they talk in a manner to excite and keep alive in the minds of the men employed in physical labour, the opinion that theirs only has a claim to the name and the rights of labour. Even when speaking not of labour, but of labourers, they hold the same levelling and depreciating language;—ascribing the rights of labour to workmen, as such, independently of all degrees of personal merit. Thus the coarsest and most ordinary labour is assumed as the standard to which all the higher degrees are adjusted; and diversity and inequality are abolished, for the supposed advantage of that which is the least and the lowest in the scale!

Do those who hold such language serve—do they even understand—the cause which they affect to advocate? Is it by such means that we can advance, or even barely keep our ground, on that glorious path of civilization in which labour acquired its proper rank and dignity? Do we not, on the contrary, mutilate, degrade, and disgrace labour, when we strip it of a part of its noblest claims, and substitute in their stead pretensions which are not only absurd and preposterous, but mean, in spite of their insolence? Lastly, does not such language show a gross misconception and violent perversion of the natural facts on which civil society in France is founded? This, though admitting unity of laws and equality of rights, assuredly never pretended to abolish that variety of faculties, merits, and destinies, which is one of the mysterious laws of God, and the inevitable result of the free will of man.

Let us now turn from civil to political society; that is, the relation existing between men, in virtue of their interests, opinions and sentiments, and the ruling power under which they live. Let us endeavour here to determine also the real and essential elements of which society is now composed in France.

In a free country, or in one struggling to become free, the elements of political society are political parties, in the widest and highest acceptation of the term.

Legally, there are now no other parties in France than those inherent in every constitutional state; the party of the Government and that of the Opposition. There are neither Legitimists nor Orleanists. The Republic exists, and will not suffer the principle of its existence to be attacked; and as this is the indisputable right of every established government, it is by no means my intention to contest or to infringe it.

But there are things so inherent in society, that prohibitive laws, even when obeyed, fail to eradicate them. There are political parties of which the germ lies so deeply buried, and the roots so widely spread, that they do not die, even when they are no longer apparent.

The Legitimist party is not a mere dynastic, nor is it a mere monarchical, party. It is indeed attached to a principle and to a name; but it also occupies a great substantive place both in the history and on the soil of France. It represents all that remains of the elements so long predominant throughout that French society which contained within itself the fruitful and vigorous germs of progress; and out of which arose, after a growth of ages, the France which suddenly burst forth in 1789, mighty, aspiring, and glorious. Though the French Revolution overthrew the ancient fabric of French society, it could not annihilate its elements. In spite of the convulsions by which they were dispersed, and in the midst of the ruins by which they are surrounded, these still subsist, and are still considerable in modern France. At every succeeding crisis they evidently acquiesce more completely in the social order and political constitution which the country has adopted; and by this acquiescence they take their station in it, and change their position without disowning their character.

Moreover, does anybody believe that the party which endeavoured to found a constitutional monarchy in 1830, and which upheld that monarchy for more than seventeen years, has vanished in the tempest that overthrew the edifice it had raised? It has been called the party of the *bourgeoisie*,—the middle classes; and this in fact it was, and still is. The ascendancy of the middle classes in France, incessantly supplied by recruits from the bulk of the population, is the characteristic feature in our history since 1789. Not only have they conquered that ascendancy, but they have justified their claims to it. Amidst the grievous errors into which they have fallen, and for which they have paid so dearly, they have shown that they really possessed the qualities that constitute the strength and greatness of a nation. On all emergencies, for all the wants of the country in war or peace, and to every kind of social career, this class has abundantly furnished men, nay, generations of men, able, active, and sincerely devoted to the service of their country. When called on in 1830 to found a new monarchy, the middle classes brought to that difficult task a spirit of justice and political sincerity of which no succeeding event can cancel the merit. In spite of all the passions and all the perils that assailed them, in spite even of their own passions, they earnestly desired constitutional order, and they faithfully observed it. At home, they respected and maintained universal, legal and practical liberty; abroad, universal, firm and prosperous peace.

I am not one of those who disregard or despise the power of the affections in political affairs. I do not regard it as any proof of greatness or strength of mind to say, "We don't care for such or such a family; we attach no value to proper names; we take men or leave them according to our wants or our interests:" to me, this language, and the class of opinions which it discloses, appear to betray far more political ignorance and impotence than elevation of mind or rectitude of judgment. It is, however, indisputable that political parties having no other attachment than that excited by proper names, and no other strength than that derived from personal affections, would be extremely feeble and inefficient. But can anybody for a moment imagine that the Legitimist party, or the party attached to the monarchy of 1830, are of that nature? Is it not evident, on the contrary, that these parties are far more the offspring of the general course of events than of attachment to persons? that they are of a social, as well as a political nature, and correspond to the most deep-rooted and indestructible elements of society in France?

Around these great parties floats the mass of the population; holding to the one or the other by its interests, its habits, or its virtuous and rational instincts; but without any strong or solid adhesion, and incessantly assailed and worked upon by Socialists and Communists of every shade. These last do not constitute political parties, for they do not espouse any political principle, nor advocate any peculiar political organization. Their only endeavour is to destroy all the influences, and to break all the ties, material or moral, which bind the part of the population living by the labour of its hands, to the class occupied in the business of the state; to divide that part of the population from the land-owner, the capitalist, the clergy, and all the other established authorities; and finally to work upon it through its miseries, and rule it by its appetites. One name denotes them all; all are members of the one great Anarchical Party. It is not the superiority of this or that form of government which they preach to the people—it is sheer and absolute anarchy; for one kind of government is as incompatible with chaos as another. There is, however, one striking fact: whether sincere or depraved, blind Utopians or designing Anarchists, all these disturbers of social order are Republicans. Not that they are more attached or more submissive to republican government than to any other; for every regular and efficient government, whether republican or monarchical, is equally odious to them; but they hope that under a republic they shall find stronger weapons to aid their attacks, and feebler barriers to resist them. This is the secret of their preference.

I have thus surveyed French society on every side. I have sought out and exhibited all its real and essential elements, and all my inquiries lead to the same result. On every side, whether in political or civil life, I meet with profound diversities and inequalities: diversities and inequalities which can neither be obliterated in civil life by unity of laws and equality of rights, nor in political life by a republican government; and which endure or revive under legislation of every kind and government of every form.

This is not an opinion, an argument, or a conjecture, but a statement of facts.

Now what is the import and tendency of these facts? Shall we find in them the ancient classifications of society? Will the ancient political denominations apply to them? Do they exhibit an aristocracy opposed to a democracy; or a nobility, a bourgeoisie, and a so-called people? Would these diversities and inequalities of social and political position form, or tend to form, a hierarchy of classes analogous to those which formerly existed in French society?

No, certainly!—the words *aristocracy, democracy, nobility, bourgeoisie,* or *hierarchy,* do not correspond to the constituent elements of modern French society, or express them with any truth or accuracy.

Does then this society consist solely of citizens equal among each other? Are there no different classes, and only individual diversities and inequalities, devoid of all political importance? Is there nothing but a great and uniform democracy, which seeks satisfaction in a republic at the risk of finding repose in a despotism?

Neither is this the fact; either of these descriptions would equally misrepresent the true state of our society. We must emancipate ourselves from the tyranny of words, and see things as they really are. France is extremely new, and yet full of the past; whilst the principles of unity and equality have determined her organization, she still contains social conditions and political situations profoundly different and unequal. There is no hierarchical classification, but there are different classes; there is no aristocracy, properly so called, but there is something which is not democracy. The real, essential, and distinct elements of French society, which I have just described, may enfeeble each other by perpetual conflicts, but neither can destroy or obliterate the other. They survive all the struggles in which they engage, and all the calamities which they inflict on each other. Their co-existence is a fact which it is not in their power to abolish. Let them then fully acquiesce in it; let them live together, and in peace. Neither the liberty nor the repose, the dignity nor the prosperity, the greatness nor the security of France, are to be had on any other terms.

On what conditions can this peace be established?

CHAPTER VI
POLITICAL CONDITIONS OF SOCIAL PEACE IN FRANCE

Whenever it shall have been distinctly perceived and fully admitted that the different classes which exist among us, and the political parties which correspond to those classes, are natural and deeply-rooted elements of French society, a great step will have been made towards social peace.

This peace is impossible so long as each of the different classes and the great political parties into which our society is divided cherishes the hope of annihilating the others, and of reigning alone. That is the evil which, ever since 1789, has periodically agitated and convulsed France. Sometimes the democratic element has aimed at the extinction of the aristocratic; at other times the aristocratic element has tried to crush the democratic, and to regain its former predominance. Constitutions, laws, and the administration of the government have been by turns directed, like engines of war, to one or the other of these ends—a war to the death, in which neither combatant believed his life compatible with that of his rival.

This war was suspended by the Emperor Napoleon. He rallied around him the classes which had formerly possessed, and those which actually enjoyed, power and influence; and by the security which he offered them, by the continual turmoil in which he kept them, or by the yoke which he imposed upon them, he established and maintained peace.

After him, from 1814 to 1830, and from 1830 to 1848, this war was renewed. A great progress had been made. Liberty had become real. Both the ancient aristocratic, and the modern democratic elements acquired strength; but though neither could succeed in suppressing the other, each was impatient of its adversary's existence, and eagerly strove for the mastery.

And now a third combatant has entered the arena. The democratic party having divided itself into two conflicting sections, the workmen are now arrayed against their masters, or the people against the middle classes. This new war, like the former, is a war to the death; for the new aspirant is as arrogant and exclusive as the others can have ever been. The sovereignty, it is said, belongs of right to the people only; and no rival, ancient or modern, noble or bourgeois, can be admitted to share it.

Every pretension of this kind must be withdrawn, not by one only, but by all of the contending parties. The great elements of society among us—the old aristocracy, the middle classes, and the people—must completely renounce the hope of excluding and annihilating each other. Let them vie with each other in influence; let each maintain its position and its rights, or even endeavour to extend and improve them, for in such efforts consists the political life of a country. But there must be an end of all radical hostility: they must resign themselves to live together, side by side, in the ranks of the government as well as in civil society. This is the first condition of social peace. How, it may be asked, can this condition be satisfied? How can the different elements of our society be brought to tolerate each other's existence, and to fulfil their several functions in the government of the country?

I reply, by such an organization of that government as may assign to each its place and functions; may concede something to the wishes, while it imposes limits to the ambition, of all.

I am here met by an idea, perhaps the most false and fatal of all those current in our days on the subject of constitutional organization. It is this:— "National unity involves political unity. There is but one people: there can exist at the head and in the name of this people, but one power."

This is the idea which most completely characterizes both revolution and despotism. The Convention and Louis XIV. exclaimed alike, "L'Etat, c'est moi."

It is as false as it is tyrannical. A nation is not a vast aggregate of men, consisting of so many thousands or millions, occupying a certain extent of ground, and concentrated in, and represented by, a unit, called king or assembly. A nation is a great organic body, formed by the union within one country of certain social elements which assume the shape and constitution naturally impressed upon them by the primitive laws of God and the free acts of man. The diversity of these elements is, as we have just seen, one of the essential facts resulting from those laws; and is absolutely inconsistent with the false and tyrannous unity which it is proposed to establish at the centre of government, as representative of that society in which it never exists.

What then, it is said, must all the elements of society, all the groups of which it is naturally composed, all the various classes, professions, and opinions it contains, be represented in the government by powers corresponding to each?

No, certainly: society is not a federation of professions, classes, and opinions, which treat, by their several delegates, of the affairs which are common to them all; any more than it is a uniform mass of exactly similar elements, which send their representatives to the centre of government only because they cannot all repair thither themselves, and are compelled to reduce themselves to a number which can meet in one place and deliberate in common. Social unity requires that there should be but one government; but the diversity of the social elements equally requires that this government should not be one sole power.

There is a natural process of attraction and concentration at work in the heart of society, and among the numberless particular associations which it contains (such as families, professions, classes, and parties), by which all the smaller associations are successively absorbed into the larger. The multitude of particular and different elements are thus reduced to a small number of principal and essential elements, which include and represent all the rest.

I do not think that these principal elements of society ought to be all specially represented in the government of the state by several authorities; I only maintain that their diversity is inconsistent with the unity of the central power.

To this reasoning it has often been confidently replied—that the various elements of society are congregated, by the process of free election, in a single assembly which represents the whole nation; and which affords them an arena for free discussion, where they can maintain their opinions, their interests and their rights, and exert their proper influence over the resolutions of the assembly, and consequently over the government of the state.

We are then to infer from this that we have discharged the claims of the most varied, weighty, and essential social elements when we have said, "Get yourselves elected, then give your opinion, and try to make it the prevalent one!" Election and discussion constitute the entire basis which is to sustain the social edifice; election and discussion afford a sufficient guarantee for all interests, rights, and liberties!

Such a theory betrays a strange ignorance of human nature, human society, and the French people.

I will put a single question. The interests of society are twofold; those of stability and conservation on the one hand, and those of activity and progress on the other. If you wanted to secure the interests of activity and progress, would you seek this security among the social elements in which the interests of stability and conservation are peculiarly strong? Undoubtedly not: you would commit the interests of activity and progress to the care of their natural and willing protectors, and you would do well. But all these various interests have equal wants and equal claims. There is no safety for any of them but in its appropriate power; that is to say, in a power analogous to it in its nature and in its relations to other powers. If the interests of stability and conservation are committed wholly to the chances of the composition of a single elective assembly, invested with the sole and final decision of all questions, and to the chances of the discussions in that assembly, be assured that sooner or later, after numerous oscillations between tyrannies of different kinds, those interests will be sacrificed or lost.

It is absurd to seek the principle of the political stability of government in the mobile elements of society. The permanent elements of society must find in the government itself, powers corresponding to them, and offering a pledge for their security. A diversity of powers is equally indispensable to conservation and to liberty.

It is matter of amazement that this truth should be disputed, for the very men who dispute it have made a great step towards its admission and application. After establishing unity of power at the head of the state, they have admitted a division of powers lower down, on account of the diversity of functions. They have carefully separated the legislative, executive, administrative, and judicial powers; thus practically acknowledging the necessity of giving guarantees to different interests, by the separation and the different constitution of these powers. How is it that they do not see that this necessity has a higher application, and that the diversity of the general interests of society and of the duties of the supreme power, imperatively requires a diversity of powers in the highest as well as in the subordinate spheres of government?

But to constitute a real and efficient diversity of powers, it is not enough that each should have a distinct place and name in the government; it is also necessary that all should be strongly organized, all fully competent to fill and to maintain the place they occupy.

It is the fashion of the day to think that harmony among the powers of the state, and security against their excess, is to be found in their weakness. People are afraid of every kind of authority; and in order to prevent their destroying each other, or encroaching upon liberty, they ingeniously endeavour to undermine them all in turn.

This is a monstrous error. Every weak power is a power doomed to perish by extinction or by usurpation. If several weak powers conflict, either one will become strong at the expense of the others, and will end in a tyranny, or they will trammel and neutralize each other, and the result will be anarchy.

What is it that has constituted the strength and success of constitutional monarchy in England? It is that, while the royalty and aristocracy were originally strong, the commonalty has become strong by successive conquests of its rights from the aristocracy and the king. Of the three constitutional powers, two retain much of their primitive greatness, and rest firmly on their deep and primæval roots; the third has risen to greatness, and has gradually struck its roots deeply into the same soil. Each is fully able to defend itself against the other, and to fulfil its peculiar mission.

When an earnest and sincere attempt was made to establish constitutional monarchy in France, its firmest adherents desired an ancient and historical basis for royalty; for the Chamber of Peers, an hereditary seat in the legislature, and for the Chamber of Deputies, direct election: not by any means in obedience to theories or precedents, but in order that the great powers of the state might be true powers,—efficient and living entities, not words or phantoms.

In the United States, notwithstanding the difference of names, situations, manners, and institutions, Washington, Hamilton, Jefferson, and Madison, when founding the Republic, recognised and acted upon the same principles. They too thought it necessary to have different powers at the head of the government; and in order that the difference might be real, they gave to each of these powers—*i.e.* the two chambers and the President—a distinct origin; as distinct as the general institutions of the country would permit, and as different as their several functions.

Diversity of origin and of nature is one of the conditions essential to the intrinsic and real strength of powers, and this again is the condition indispensable to political harmony and social peace.

Nor is it only at the summit and centre of government that these principles ought to guide the organization of power; they are equally applicable through the whole extent of the country, in the management of its local, no less than of its general affairs. A great deal has been said in favour of centralization and administrative unity, and there is no doubt that they have rendered great service to France. We shall preserve many of their forms, regulations, maxims, and works; but the time of their sovereignty is past. Centralization is no longer sufficient for the chief wants and pressing dangers of society. The struggle is no longer confined to the centre; it agitates the whole nation. Since property, family, and all the bases of society, are attacked everywhere, they must everywhere be vigorously defended; and functionaries or orders which have to travel from the centre of government will be found a very inadequate defence, even though supported by bayonets. Landed proprietors, and heads of families, who are the natural guardians of society, must all be enjoined and empowered to maintain its security by conducting its affairs: they must have an active share in the management of its local as well as its general interests; in the administration, as well as the government of the country: the central government ought to uphold the banner of social order, but it cannot bear the whole burthen of it unaided.

I speak always on the presumption that I am speaking *to* a free country, and *of* a free government; for it is under free governments that the safety of society demands all these conditions: they have evidently no application to absolute governments.

Absolute power is, however, subject to certain conditions, as well as liberty. It is far from being always possible where it would be submitted to, nor can it be obtained wherever it is desired.

Let the friends of freedom never forget that nations prefer absolute power to anarchy. The first want—the first instinct—of communities, as well as of governments or of individuals, is self-preservation. Now a community may exist under absolute power; under anarchy, if it lasts, it must perish.

The readiness, I might almost say the eagerness, with which nations throw their liberties into the gulf of anarchy, in the desperate attempt to close it, is a shameful spectacle. I know nothing more lamentable to witness than this sudden renunciation of all the rights so noisily and vehemently demanded. The friend of freedom and of progress who would fall into despair of man and of the future at this humiliating sight must withdraw into himself, and refresh and invigorate his soul at those high and pure fountains which nourish deep convictions and far-reaching hopes.

Let not France, whatever be her peril, reckon on absolute power to save her. It would not justify her confidence. In her ancient society, absolute power reposed on a principle of moderation and of permanence; while, under the Emperor Napoleon, it contained a principle of strength, either of which it would vainly seek for now. Popular tyranny or military dictatorship may be the expedient of a day, but can never be a form of government. Free institutions are now as necessary to social peace as they are to individual dignity; and power, whatever be its nature or origin, whether republican or monarchical, has no wiser course to pursue than to learn to use them, for they are now its only instruments and its only stay.

If some are tempted to seek repose in other sources, let them abandon all such hopes. Whatever be the future destiny of France, we shall not escape from the necessity of a constitutional government; we are condemned, for our own salvation, to surmount all the difficulties, and to fulfil all the conditions, with which it may be encumbered.

There is but one means of rendering ourselves equal to this mighty task, and of complying with this imperious necessity. All the elements of stability, all the conservative forces in the country must unite closely and act constantly together. It is no more possible to extinguish democracy in the nation than liberty in the government. That immense movement which has been communicated to every country and agitates all their deepest recesses; which is incessantly inciting every class and every individual to think, to desire, to claim, to act, to employ his activity in every direction,—this movement will not be stopped. It is a fact in which we must acquiesce, whether it pleases or displeases us, whether it awakens our fears or excites our hopes. But though we cannot extinguish this movement, we can guide and govern it; and if it is not guided and governed, it will throw back the whole current of civilization, and will be the opprobrium as well as the curse of humanity. Democracy, to be guided and governed, must form a considerable ingredient in the state, but it must not be the sole one: it must be strong enough to climb itself, but never to pull down others: it must find issues, and encounter barriers on every side. Democracy is a fertilizing, but muddy stream, whose waters are never beneficent till the turbid and impetuous current has spread itself abroad and subsided into calmness and purity.

The Dutch, a great people, though in a small country, whose republican glory shone brightly even amidst the full blaze of the monarchical glory of Louis XIV., conquered their country from the ocean, and maintained their conquest, by cutting canals and raising dikes on every side. It is the ceaseless care of the whole community that the canals be never obstructed and the dikes never broken; for on this depend the prosperity and the existence of Holland.

Let all the conservative elements of France learn from this example; let them unite all their efforts, let them keep a common and incessant watch, that the rising tide of democracy may always find safe channels and indestructible barriers. On the joint and efficient action of these depend the safety of the community, and the safety of each individual composing it. If the conservative elements of French society know how to combine and to form a united body, if the party spirit which prevails among them shall give way to a large and enlightened political spirit, then France, and the democracy of France, are saved. If the conservative elements remain disunited and disorganized, Democracy will destroy France, and will perish under the ruins she has made.

CHAPTER VII
MORAL CONDITIONS OF SOCIAL PEACE IN FRANCE

The political conditions which I have just specified are indispensable to the re-establishment of social peace in France; but they alone will not suffice. Such a work requires something more than a good organization of powers; it requires a certain measure of prudence and virtue on the part of the people themselves. It is a gross delusion to believe in the sovereign power of political machinery. The free will of man plays a great part in social affairs, and the success of institutions must in the end depend on the men who live under them.

Much has lately been said about Christianity, and the name of Jesus Christ has been frequently introduced into the harangues of demagogues. God forbid that I should suffer my mind to dwell long on these profanations,—this hideous mixture of cynicism and hypocrisy. I shall only suggest one question—If the French nation were sincerely and practically Christian, what would be its conduct in the midst of the terrible difficulties by which it is agitated and perplexed?

The rich and great of the earth would earnestly and perseveringly labour to alleviate the distresses of those beneath them. Their intercourse with the poorer classes would be active, affectionate, morally and physically beneficent. The various sufferings and perils of humanity would call forth corresponding associations, endowments, and works of charity.

The poor and humble would be submissive to the will of God and the laws of society. They would seek the satisfaction of their wants in regular and assiduous labour, the improvement of their condition in good conduct and provident habits, and consolation and hope in the futurity promised to man.

These are the Christian virtues—they are called Faith, Hope, and Charity. Is this the conduct men are exhorted by the preachers of Democracy to pursue? Are these the sentiments which these men, who affect a veneration for the Founder of Christianity, try to rekindle in the hearts of the people?

I doubt whether they can carry the impudence of mendacity so far as to answer in the affirmative; and if they dared to do so, I am sure that, spite of the credulity of the public, they would receive a universal contradiction.

But these monstrous attempts, whether the result of fraud or of folly, will not succeed. Christianity will not be disfigured or degraded so. Nothing can be more anti-Christian than the ideas, the language, or the influence of the present race of reformers of social order. If Communism and Socialism prevailed, Christianity must become extinct: if Christianity were more potent, Communism and Socialism would soon sink into the chaotic mass of obscure and forgotten extravagances.

I wish to be perfectly just; and while attacking notions which are the disgrace and the curse of our times, I would acknowledge whatever germ of morality they contain, and show what virtuous pretexts or benevolent instincts may delude their advocates or seduce their converts.

There is a sentiment, noble and beautiful in itself, which has been much and often appealed to throughout all the perturbations and convulsions of society in France; this sentiment is, enthusiasm for mankind—the enthusiasm of confidence, sympathy, and hope. This feeling reigned supreme among us in 1789, and gave its resistless impulse to that epoch. There was no virtue that was not ascribed to man—no success that was not hoped and predicted for him. Faith and hope in man took the place of faith and hope in God. The trial was not long deferred. The idol did not long retain its power. Confidence was soon convicted of presumption, and sympathy ended in social war and the scaffold. The hopes that were fulfilled appeared insignificant, compared to those that had vanished like dreams. Never did experience advance with such rapid strides to confront and overthrow pride.

Yet it is to this same sentiment that our modern reformers of social order appeal. It is this same idolatrous enthusiasm for human nature that they invoke. At the same time that they rob man of his sublimest emotions and loftiest prospects, they exalt without measure his nature and his power: rather, I ought to say, they miserably degrade them, for they promise him nothing beyond this earth; but while there, their belief in him is blind and implicit—their hope from him, and for him, boundless.

The most melancholy reflection is, that this insane idolatry is their only excuse; the only one of their ideas which springs from a source of the smallest elevation, or possesses the smallest moral value. If they had not a blind faith in man, and a servile adoration of humanity, they would be nothing more than the propagators of a rapacious, brutish, and lawless materialism.

"If man exalteth himself," says Pascal, "I abase him; if he abaseth himself, I exalt him." We ought continually to bear in mind and to apply these admirable words. Certainly man is a being worthy to inspire us with respect and love, and with high hopes of his future condition. To those who were insensible to the nobleness of his nature and his destiny—to himself, if he forgot it—I should say with Pascal, "If man abaseth himself, I exalt him." But to those who promise themselves everything from him, by promising him everything; whose expectations from him are as boundless as those they labour to excite in him; to those who, goaded by their own pride, are constantly striving to inflate his pride; who forget, and try to make him forget, the frailty and wretchedness of his nature, the supreme laws by which he is bound, and the support of which he stands in need,—to those men I would say with Pascal, "If man exalteth himself, I abase him." And facts,—recent, glaring, incontrovertible facts,—say it far more impressively than I.

It is impossible to restore France to the state of things which prevailed in 1789—to rekindle that enthusiasm of presumptuous confidence and hope with which the nation was then drunk—an enthusiasm which then was genuine as well as general, had the ardour and spontaneity of youth, and was rendered excusable by inexperience, but which now would be only a false and factitious excitement; a thin, an ineffectual veil thrown over bad passions and insane dreams. By what incurable arrogance could we reject the lessons which God has lavished upon us for the last sixty years? He does not require of us to despair of ourselves and of our species, to abandon all efforts for its progress, or to shut our hearts against a tender sympathy in its weal or woe; but He does forbid us to exalt our own nature into an idol. He commands us to see it as it is; without illusion and without coldness; and to love and serve it according to the laws He has established. I have certainly no desire to extinguish any of the small portion of moral ardour still remaining in the world, nor to infuse additional doubt and indifference into hearts already so lukewarm and uncertain. But neither can I add to their delusions. It is not by retracing its course toward the sources of the revolution, that France will walk with a firm and animated step: those fountains are all dry, and our generation will not go to slake its thirst or refresh its spirit at them. You complain of its languor; you want to see the faith and the moral energy, which are the soul and strength of nations, revive among us: but it is vain to seek them in the revolutionary spirit, which is wholly incapable of inspiring them. It is a fire which has still power to consume, but can neither warm nor enlighten. Instead of reviving and invigorating our belief in the great truths which are the wholesome stimulants as well as the true guardians of society, they can only diffuse doubt and perplexity. Certainly France wants to be morally elevated and strengthened; she wants to regain her faith in, and attachment to, fixed and undisputed principles. But the revolutionary spirit can do nothing to appease these wants; the scenes and the harangues, the predictions and the recollections which it suggests, can only retard the work. The honour of its accomplishment is reserved for other moral powers and other intellectual tendencies.

Among the foremost, are the domestic sentiments and morals. The Family is now, more than ever, the first element and the last rampart of society. Whilst, in general society, everything becomes more and more mobile, personal, and transient, it is in domestic life that the demand for permanency, and the feeling of the necessity of sacrificing the present to the future, are indestructible. It is in domestic life that the ideas and the virtues which form a counterpoise to the excessive and ungoverned movement excited in the great centres of civilization, are formed. The tumult of business and pleasure, temptation and strife which reigns in our great cities, would soon throw the whole of society into a deplorable state of ferment and dissolution, if domestic life, with its calm activity, its permanent interests, and its fixed property, did not oppose solid barriers throughout the country to the restless waves of this stormy sea. It is in the bosom of domestic life, and under its influences, that private, the basis of public, morality is most securely maintained. There too, and in our days there almost exclusively, the affections of our nature, — friendship, gratitude, and self-devotion, — all the ties which unite hearts in the sense of a common destiny, grow and flourish. The time has been when, under other forms of society, these private affections found a place in public life; when devoted attachments strengthened political connexions. These times are past, never to return. In the vast and complicated and ever-moving society of our days, general interests and principles, the sentiments of the masses, and the combinations of parties, have the entire possession and direction of public life. The private affections are ties too delicate to exercise any powerful influence over the conflicts of that pitiless field. But it is never without serious injury that one of the vital elements of human nature is uprooted out of any of the fields of human action; and the complete absence of tender and faithful attachments in that almost exclusive domain of abstract ideas and general or selfish interests, has robbed political life of a noble ornament and a great source of strength. It is of incalculable importance to society that there should be some safe retreat in which the affectionate dispositions — I would almost say passions — of the heart of man may expand in freedom; and that, occasionally emerging from that retreat, they may exhibit their presence and their power by some beautiful examples in that tumultuous region of politics in which they are so rarely found. But these social virtues must be nursed in the bosom of domestic life; these social affections must spring from family affections. Home, the abode of stability and morality, also contains the hearth at which all our affections and all our self-devotion are kindled; it is in the circle of the Family that the noblest parts of our nature find satisfactions they would seek for else in vain; it is from that circle that, when circumstances demand, they can go forth to adorn and bless society.

Next to the spirit of family, the political spirit is that from which France has now the greatest services to expect, and which she ought to foster with the greatest care. The political spirit shows itself in the will and the power to take a regular and active part in public affairs, without employment of violence or risk of disturbance. The greater the spread and cultivation of the political spirit, the more does it teach men the necessity and the habit of seeing things as they are in their exact and naked truth. To see, not what exists, but what they wish; to indulge complacently in illusions about facts, as if facts would, with equal complacency, take the form that they desire,— is the radical and characteristic weakness of men still new to political life, and the source of their most fatal errors. To see things as they are, is the first and very excellent fruit of the political spirit, and gives birth to another not less excellent, viz.—that, by learning to see only what is, we learn to desire only what is possible; the exact appreciation of facts begets moderation in designs and pretensions. The political spirit, true and sincere to itself, becomes prudent and reasonable towards others. Nothing inclines men more to moderation than a full knowledge of the truth; for it is rarely that she throws all her weight into one scale. The political spirit is thus naturally led by prudence, if by no higher morality, to that respect for rights which is not only its fundamental law and essential merit, but the sole basis of social stability; since, where law ceases, nothing remains but force, which is essentially variable and precarious. The respect for rights supposes, or produces, the respect for law, the habitual source of rights. The real and the possible, rights and law, such are the subjects upon which the political spirit is constantly exercised, and which become the habitual objects of its inquiry and its veneration. It thus maintains, or re-establishes, a moral principle of fixity in the relations of individuals, and a moral principle of authority in those of the state.

The more the value for family ties shall increase at the expense of the selfishness of an isolated existence, and the more the political shall gain upon the revolutionary spirit, the more tranquil will the society of France become, and the more firmly will it rest upon its foundations.

Nevertheless, neither the domestic nor the political spirit would suffice for the task. They need the assistance of another and a higher spirit, whose influence penetrates more deeply than they can do into the human soul. It is peculiar to religion that she has a language for every individual; a language which all can understand, the high as well as the humble, the happy as well as the unhappy; and that she ascends or descends, without an effort, into every rank and region of society. And it is one of the admirable features of the constitution of the Christian church, that her ministers are not only scattered over, but form an integral part of, the whole of society; living as near to the cottage as the palace; in habitual and intimate intercourse with the highest and the lowest; equally the monitors of greatness and the consolers of misery. This tutelary power, spite of the abuses and the faults into which it has been led by its very force and extent, has for ages exercised a more vigilant and energetic control over the moral dignity and the dearest interests of man, than any other. Nobody would be so averse as I should, for the sake of religion herself, to see a revival of the abuses by which she has been disfigured or corrupted; but I confess that I do not fear this at the present day. The principles of lay supremacy and freedom of thought have definitively triumphed in modern society: they may still have some enemies to repel, and some conflicts to sustain, but their victory is certain; they have in their favour the prevailing institutions, manners, opinions, and passions; and that general and overwhelming current of ideas and events which flows on through all diversities, obstacles, and perils, in the same direction, at Rome, Madrid, Turin, Berlin, and Vienna, no less than at London or Paris. For modern society to fear religion, or to dispute her influence with acrimony, would therefore be a puerile alarm and a fatal error. You are surrounded by an immense and excited multitude; you complain that you want means to act upon it, to enlighten, direct, control, and tranquillize it; that you have little intercourse with these men, save through the tax-gatherer and the policeman; that they are given over, without defence, to the inflammatory declamations of charlatans and demagogues, and to the blind violence of their own passions. Dispersed among them, you have men whose express mission and constant occupation it is to guide their faith, to console their distresses, to show them their duties, to awaken and elevate their hopes, to exercise over them that moral influence which you vainly seek elsewhere. And would you not second these men in their work, when they can second you so powerfully in yours, precisely in those obscure enclosures where you so rarely penetrate, and where the enemies of social order enter continually, and sap all their foundations?

There is, it is true, a condition attached to the favour and the political efficacy of the religious spirit; it demands sincere respect, and liberty. I will even confess that the fears and desires of the religious party often render them unjust, captious, suspicious, rancorous, and exacting; that they sometimes fall into the vortex of those false, anarchical and chimerical ideas which it is their peculiar vocation to combat. I will make as large concessions as can be required, as to the injustice you must expect to submit to, and the precautions you will have to take; yet I shall say at the conclusion, as I said at the beginning, Do not hold up acrimonious disputes with religion; do not fear her influences; allow them space and liberty to expand and to act in the largest and most powerful manner. On the whole, they will certainly be more in favour of tranquillity than of strife, and will assist more than they will embarrass you.

If we were under that proximate necessity of acting, which affords a light indispensable to those who want to do more than lay down general principles of action, it would be our business to inquire by what practical means, by what positive institutions or laws, the domestic, the political, and the religious spirit might be duly strengthened and developed in our country. At present I shall only add one word. We cannot treat with great moral forces as if they were mercenary and suspected auxiliaries. They exist by themselves, with their natural merits and defects, their unavoidable benefits and dangers. We must accept them, such as they are; without pretending to be either their slaves or their tyrants, without giving up everything to them, but also without trying to withhold their just portion. The religious, the domestic, and the political spirit are more than ever beneficent, more than ever necessary, in our society. Neither social tranquillity, nor stability, nor order can dispense with their co-operation. Seek then that co-operation with sincerity; receive it with a good grace, and resign yourselves to pay the price of it.

Societies, no more than individuals, are exempted from the necessity of purchasing advantages by efforts and sacrifices.

CHAPTER VIII
CONCLUSION

Let not France deceive herself. Not all the experiments she may try, not all the revolutions she may make, or suffer to be made, will ever emancipate her from the necessary and inevitable conditions of social tranquillity and good government. She may refuse to admit them, and may suffer without measure or limit from her refusal, but she cannot escape from them.

We have tried everything:—Republic—Empire—Constitutional Monarchy. We are beginning our experiments anew. To what must we ascribe their ill success? In our own times, before our own eyes, in three of the greatest nations in the world, these three same forms of government—Constitutional Monarchy in England, the Empire in Russia, and the Republic in North America—endure and prosper. Have we the monopoly of all impossibilities?

Yes; so long as we remain in the chaos in which we are plunged, in the name, and by the slavish idolatry, of Democracy; so long as we can see nothing in society but Democracy, as if that were its sole ingredient; so long as we seek in government nothing but the domination of Democracy, as if that alone had the right and the power to govern.

On these terms the Republic is equally impossible as the Constitutional Monarchy, and the Empire, as the Republic; for all regular and stable government is impossible.

And liberty—legal and energetic liberty—is no less impossible than stable and regular government.

The world has seen great and illustrious communities reduced to this deplorable condition; incapable of supporting any legal and energetic liberty, or any regular and stable government; condemned to interminable and sterile political oscillations, from the various shades and forms of anarchy to the equally various forms of despotism. For a heart capable of any feeling of pride or dignity, I cannot conceive a more cruel suffering than to be born in such an age. Nothing remains but to retire to the sanctuary of domestic life, and the prospects of religion. The joys and the sacrifices, the labours and the glories of public life exist no more.

Such is not, God be praised, the state of France; such will not be the closing scene of her long and glorious career of civilization,—of all her exertions, conquests, hopes, and sufferings. France is full of life and vigour. She has not mounted so high, to descend in the name of equality to so low a level. She possesses the elements of a good political organization. She has numerous classes of citizens, enlightened and respected, already accustomed to manage the business of their country, or prepared to undertake it. Her soil is covered with an industrious and intelligent population, who detest anarchy, and ask only to live and to labour in peace. There is an abundance of virtue in the bosoms of her families, and of good feeling in the hearts of her sons. We have wherewithal to struggle against the evil that devours us. But the evil is immense. There are no words wherein to describe, no measure wherewith to measure it. The suffering and the shame it inflicts upon us are slight, compared to those it prepares for us if it endures. And who will say that it cannot endure, when all the passions of the wicked, all the extravagances of the mad, all the weaknesses of the good, concur to foment it? Let all the sane forces of France then unite to combat it. They will not be too many, and they must not wait till it is too late. Their united strength will more than once bend under the weight of their work, and France, ere she can be saved, will still need to pray that God would protect her.

9 789361 150951